# CONTEMPORARY ISSUES

# EDUCATION

# CONTEMPORARY ISSUES

CRIMINAL JUSTICE SYSTEM
EDUCATION
THE ENVIRONMENT
GENDER EQUALITY
GUN CONTROL
HEALTH CARE
IMMIGRATION
JOBS AND ECONOMY
MENTAL HEALTH
POVERTY AND WELFARE
PRIVACY AND SOCIAL MEDIA
RACE RELATIONS
RELIGIOUS FREEDOM

# CONTEMPORARY ISSUES

# EDUCATION

ASHLEY NICOLE

## MASON CREST
PHILADELPHIA | MIAMI

## MASON CREST

450 Parkway Drive, Suite D, Broomall, Pennsylvania 19008
(866) MCP-BOOK (toll-free) • www.masoncrest.com

© 2020 by Mason Crest, an imprint of National Highlights, Inc.

Printed and bound in the United States of America.

CPSIA Compliance Information: Batch #CCRI2019.
For further information, contact Mason Crest at 1-866-MCP-Book.

First printing
1 3 5 7 9 8 6 4 2

ISBN (hardback) 978-1-4222-4389-3
ISBN (series) 978-1-4222-4387-9
ISBN (ebook) 978-1-4222-7404-0

Library of Congress Cataloging-in-Publication Data
on file at the Library of Congress

Interior and cover design: Torque Advertising + Design
Production: Michelle Luke

Publisher's Note: Websites listed in this book were active at the time of publication. The publisher is not responsible for websites that have changed their address or discontinued operation since the date of publication. The publisher reviews and updates the websites each time the book is reprinted.

# QR CODES AND LINKS TO THIRD-PARTY CONTENT

# CONTENTS

Chapter 1: Education in the United States ................................... 7

Chapter 2: Can the Education System Be Reformed? ................29

Chapter 3: Is Common Core Curriculum Effective? ..................49

Chapter 4: Do Charter Schools Benefit Students? ...................67

Chapter 5: Is Standardized Testing Ruining Education? ..........83

Series Glossary of Key Terms ............................................. 101

Further Reading ................................................................. 102

Internet Resources ............................................................ 103

Chapter Notes .................................................................. 104

Organizations to Contact ................................................... 108

Index ............................................................................... 109

Author's Biography and Credits .......................................... 112

## KEY ICONS TO LOOK FOR:

**Words to Understand:** These words with their easy-to-understand definitions will increase the reader's understanding of the text while building vocabulary skills.

**Sidebars:** This boxed material within the main text allows readers to build knowledge, gain insights, explore possibilities, and broaden their perspectives by weaving together additional information to provide realistic and holistic perspectives.

**Educational videos:** Readers can view videos by scanning our QR codes, providing them with additional educational content to supplement the text. Examples include news coverage, moments in history, speeches, iconic sports moments, and much more!

**Text-Dependent Questions:** These questions send the reader back to the text for more careful attention to the evidence presented there.

**Research Projects:** Readers are pointed toward areas of further inquiry connected to each chapter. Suggestions are provided for projects that encourage deeper research and analysis.

**Series Glossary of Key Terms:** This back-of-the-book glossary contains terminology used throughout this series. Words found here increase the reader's ability to read and comprehend higher-level books and articles in this field.

## WORDS TO UNDERSTAND

**bipartisan**—cooperation or agreement between two
political parties that typically oppose each other.

**compulsory**—obligated, coerced, or required by law or rule.

**curriculum**—basic learning standards or guidelines.

**de facto segregation**—racial segregation that happens
by fact rather than by law. Schools may be racially
segregated based on the students that live near each
school.

# EDUCATION IN
# THE UNITED STATES

# CHAPTER 1

Each year, about 56.6 million children attend elementary and secondary schools in the United States. Most of these students attend public schools, though options like private school, charter school, and homeschool are available. About 3.6 million of these students will graduate from high school at the end of the current school year. In addition, more than 20 million students attend either a two-year or four-year college or institution of higher education.

Attending school is **compulsory** for children in the United States, though each state establishes its own laws regarding curriculum and learning standards, truancy and absenteeism, and homeschooling. The conflict between national oversight and state rule is an ongoing issue in America's schools. For example, does the federal government have the right to issue a standardized **curriculum** for all public schools? Do states have the right to localize standardized testing? Moral and legal issues arise even in discussions of public education.

The United States has more than 13,600 school districts encompassing more than 98,000 schools, including charter schools. Additionally, the country boasts more than 34,000 private schools. Some students attend school at home, or take online education courses. School choice is one of the biggest educational concerns facing Americans today. Parents want to know they are sending their child to a school that provides them every opportunity to achieve more.

The United States spends more money per student on education than any other country. However, on Pearson Learning's Global Education Index, a ranking of the educational quality provided by each country, the United States is not among the top countries. The most recent version of the Global Education Index, published in 2016, shows Japan, South Korea, Hong Kong, and Singapore atop the rankings, with the United States at number fourteen. Many people are unimpressed when they consider the expenditures associated with education in the nation. Education reform advocates consistently look for new ways to improve the nation's school systems, but the road ahead presents many challenges.

Scan here to learn more about public versus private schools.

# CLASSROOMS IN THE UNITED STATES

Each state's government sets the standards for its public schools, which receive state and local government funding to operate. Private schools, on the other hand, have greater freedom to determine their curriculum, educational programs, staffing needs, and regional accreditation. Accreditation is a process by which school practices are reviewed by an independent expert authority, to make sure they are properly preparing students to move up to the next educational level. (from middle school to high school, for example, or from high school to college, or from college to graduate school). Most states have laws requiring or encouraging accreditation for public schools and state-chartered private schools.

Homeschooling is another option for students. One of the biggest reasons parents choose homeschooling is concern about the public school environment. They may feel that public schools are unsafe or that the children attending the school misbehave. Other reasons parents homeschool include a desire to pursue religious curriculum and dissatisfaction with the curriculum of public institutions. The United States recognizes homeschooling as a valid means of obtaining an education, though state-level laws apply.

By and large, public schooling is the most popular way to achieve an education in the United States. Public schools typically include grades kindergarten through twelfth grade, each year progressing in difficulty and ex-

*One goal of modern-day education is to prepare students for a fulfilling and productive career in a field that interests them.*

pectations. After four years of high school, students should be prepared with basic skills that they will need to enroll in college, enlist in the military, or enter the workforce.

Primary school typically encompasses kindergarten through sixth grade with some slight variations in grade level. Common Core-based curricula are a common staple in primary school classrooms, which typically contain between 20 and 30 students. These schools typically focus on basic arithmetic, algebra, English, and fundamentals of science, history, and the arts.

Secondary education, which encompasses middle school (or junior high) and high school, typically involves an emphasis on topics like science, math, language, and social studies. Students typically move from classroom to classroom in secondary school, with each teacher focusing on a different subject.

Television shows often depict the American classroom, demonstrating exactly how much of a role education plays in the lives of young people across the nation. For many, the classroom is more than just a place for academic learning. It's also a place for socialization and creativity.

*"Education is the most powerful weapon which you can use to change the world."*[1]
*—Nelson Mandela*

# THE ORIGINS OF PUBLIC EDUCATION

American colonists valued education, but they often lacked the resources necessary to send their children to school. For many children, school was not considered necessary. For the most part, parents taught their children how to read at home. A system of apprenticeship, in which young people were sent to work with a skilled craftsman at an early age so that they would learn the trade, was another key component of colonial education.

The Massachusetts Bay colony led the way in public education, largely because Puritan religious leaders wanted to make sure that colonists could read the Bible. The Boston Latin School, founded in 1635, was the first public school established in the United States. The school was supported by donations, rather than from local taxes. The first college in the colonies was Harvard, founded in 1636. During the 1640s, the Massachusetts Bay colony passed laws that required each town in the colony to establish and pay to operate public schools. Other British colonies, particularly in the North, soon followed this example.

At first, early American schools in the northern colonies were only open to boys and young men from white families. Eventually, girls were given the opportunity to attend primary schools, although it was extremely rare for young women to receive higher education. Education was much different in the southern states, where the populations were more rural. There were few schools in the South. Wealthy families hired tutors to teach their children at

NOAH WEBSTER
"The Schoolmaster of the Republic"

*Today Noah Webster (1758–1843) is known for the dictionary that carries his name. But in the late eighteenth century Webster's textbooks were widely used in American schools. This commemorative print made after his death calls Webster the "Schoolmaster of the Republic."*

home; those parents who could not afford a tutor taught their children to read and write themselves.

The public education system changed after the American Revolution. Leaders in the newly established federal

*Reforms proposed and implemented by Horace Mann (1796-1859) changed the way that public education was provided in the United States.*

government sought ways to unify the country and create a common American culture. Education became part of the plan to create a sense of community. Schools throughout the new United States began used new textbooks that created a new standard of spelling and implemented notions of patriotism and religion. Still, most school students came from wealthier families. In fact, many educational opportunities were available only to those of upper-class standing at this time.

It was not until the mid-1800s that stronger calls for free, compulsory education began. Many reasons existed for this change. During the nineteenth century the US economy moved from largely agricultural to highly industrialized. There was a growing need for men and women who could read, write, and perform math. And with waves of immigrants coming from Europe, the government also wanted to teach about the country's history and desired standards of behavior.

One of the most important educational reformers during the first half of the nineteenth century was Horace Mann. He wanted teachers to be better trained, and proposed that curriculum should become more standard among schools. He believed that public schools should accept students of all social classes, and should teach them certain values. Mann's reforms included grouping students

*Mount Holyoke College in Massachusetts was founded in 1837 as a place where women could receive a college education. Before this time, there were few opportunities for female students.*

together in grades based on their ages. His work between the years of 1837 and 1859 shaped the foundation of the modern American educational system.

## CONTINUING TO CHANGE

The educational system continued to change after the Civil War. Tax-supported schools and educational institutions were established throughout the Southern states. Most schools were segregated, with black and white students attending separate facilities. Often, the schools for white

*African-American students attend a history class at the Tuskegee Institute, circa 1900. The Tuskegee Institute in Alabama was established in 1881 by former slaves Booker T. Washington and Lewis Adams as a place to educate black teachers.*

*"Education is an important element in the struggle for human rights. It is the means to help our children and our people rediscover their identity and thereby increase their self-respect. Education is our passport to the future, for tomorrow belongs only to the people who prepare for it today."[2]*

*—Malcom X*

students were better funded and equipped than the schools for black students. This was true not only in the Southern states, but throughout most of the United States. To serve the needs of African-American students, black colleges like Howard University in Washington, D.C., Spelman College in Atlanta, or the Tuskegee Institute in Alabama were established in the 1870s and 1880s.

During the early twentieth century, the number of private schools and colleges grew in the United States, especially in rural parts of the country. Where education once ended after eighth grade, by the 1940s more than half of all students were graduating from high school.

The American educational system continued to change

after World War II. In 1954, the Supreme Court ruled in *Brown v. Board of Education of Topeka, Kansas* that segregation of public schools was unconstitutional. The Court

## SPECIAL EDUCATION IN AMERICA

The United States did not officially educate children with disabilities until the 1960s. Until this point, families of children with disabilities had to educate the child themselves or pay for private tutoring at home. In the 1950s, advocacy groups for children with special needs were established by parents who demanded their voices be heard and their children receive education.

It was not until 1975 that special education programs became a mandatory component of the public school system in the United States. That year, Congress passed the Education for All Handicapped Children Act (EAHCA). In 1990, the federal government added more programs under the Individuals with Disabilities Education Act (IDEA).

Under this legislation, students are entitled to an education that is appropriate for their abilities. There are more than a dozen different categories of disability, including hearing impairment, traumatic brain injuries, autism, language disability, and behavioral disability.

ordered that schools be desegregated "with all deliber-ate speed." However, at times intervention by the federal government was required to make Southern school districts comply. Today, segregation of schools on the basis of race remains illegal.

Schools in the northern region of the country had be-come segregated in a different way, as blacks were exclud-

One of the biggest issues the cost of accommodating students with special needs. Government funding ensures that these students receive accommodations, whether they be wheelchair-accessible buildings or educators who specialize in special education.

Today, special education often begins with development of an individualized education plan, or IEP. Whenever possible, children with special needs are integrated into regular classrooms, sometimes receiving help from a trained aide. In other cases, students with IEPs are pulled out of the classroom to work with a special education teacher in an individual or small group setting. Special education can also involve occupational, speech, or physical therapy.

Special education is a crucial component of our educational system today. About 14 percent of American schoolchildren—roughly 6.7 million students—are enrolled in special education programs in the United States, according to the National Center for Education Statistics.

*Despite the Supreme Court's* Brown v. Board of Education *ruling, many communities resisted school integration. The federal government sometimes had to send the National Guard to enforce the law. Here a guardsman watches as black students enter a high school in Tennessee.*

ed from certain residential neighborhoods. Attempts to reduce this **de facto** segregation occurred during the 1960s and 1970s, with students being bused out of their neighborhoods to attend different schools. Many parents did not approve of busing students to different schools, and there were frequent protests.

In 1965, the administration of President Lyndon B. Johnson focused its efforts on improving the lives of those living in poverty. One of Johnson's proposals was the Elementary and Secondary Education Act, which provided funding for public schools, implemented standardized testing, and prevented the establishment of a national curriculum. Other legislation supported by Johnson was the Higher Education Act of 1965, which created funding that would help high school graduates pursue higher education (now known as Pell Grants).

During the 1970s, changes included special education reforms in public schools. In the past, students with disabilities

*President George W. Bush championed the 2002 No Child Left Behind Act, which increased the federal government's role in public education.*

had been largely ignored by the public education system. Passage of the Education for All Handicapped Children Act ensured that students with special needs would be accommodated in public schools.

In recent years, federal government programs have attempted to create accountability for schools. In 2002,

Congress passed the No Child Left Behind Act (NCLB) with **bipartisan** support. This program sought to implement measures that would penalize schools that failed to meet certain benchmarks set by the state governments, or failed to address achievement gaps among different schools. In

*Parents and students attend a middle school science fair. In recent years, school districts have placed greater emphasis on science, technology, engineering, and math programs.*

2015, NCLB was replaced by a new initiative, the Every Student Succeeds Act. President Barack Obama also created a stimulus package that provided $100 billion for public schools.

Another recent development is the increasing focus on STEM (Science, Technology, Engineering, and Math) curriculum. Under the Obama administration, STEM programs received a boost in federal funding. "Though the United States has historically been a leader in these fields, fewer students have been focusing on these topics recently," writes Elaine J. Horn. "According to the US Department of Education, only 16 percent of high school students are interested in a STEM career and have proven a proficiency in mathematics. . . . The goal is to get American students from the middle of the pack in science and math to the top of the pack in the international arena."[3]

In addition, schools today are taking on roles that extend beyond the teaching of skills like reading and arithmetic. They investigate reports of threats, harassment, and bullying, and work with local authorities when such problems occur. Most schools have also implemented character education programs, which are meant to teach young people critical values such as respect, fairness, and the importance of being a good citizens. Schools have always been involved in teaching values, but some parents today believe the current character education programs reach into areas that should be the responsibility of families or religious groups. Other parents expect schools to intervene

Connecticut students take part in a March for Our Lives anti-gun rally in Hartford in March 2018. A rash of school shootings during 2018, in places like Parkland, Florida, and Santa Fe, Texas, raised concerns about student safety.

even more through character education.

## SCHOOL SAFETY IN THE UNITED STATES

One of the biggest concerns parents have about sending their children to school today is safety. Since the start of 2009, there have been nearly 300 school shootings. One of the worst of these occurred on February 14, 2018, when a nineteen-year-old named Nikolas Cruz killed fourteen students and three teachers, and wounded seventeen others, with an AR-15 rifle at Marjory Stoneman Douglas High School in Parkland, Florida. A few months later, in May 2018, a seventeen-year-old student named Dimitrios Pagourtzis killed ten people and wounded thirteen others at Santa Fe High School in a suburb of Houston, Texas.

An August 2018 poll conducted by the Gallup Organization found that 35 percent of parents feared for their child's safety when they were in school. However, statistically speaking the likelihood that a student will be hurt or killed in a public school is extremely low.

School districts have reacted to the rise in school shootings by implementing new security measures. These can be very expensive: for example, the Baltimore County public school system spent $10 million on security cameras over a five-year period. Other schools undergo costly renovations to make their facilities safer, such as creating vestibules to manage the flow of visitors, or eliminating modular trailers that students must leave the school building to access. Hiring a school resource officer—a police officer who works in a school, building relationships with students and providing security as needed—can cost a school district $120,000 a year or more. Schools also spend money and time developing emergency response plans, practicing evacuation or "shelter in place" drills, and providing mental health screening to identify potentially troubled students early.

Some states have sought to lower the cost of adding a police presence in schools. In 2016, for example, New Jersey created a program of Class III special law enforcement officers who could only work in schools. These positions are open to experienced officers who have recently retired from a police department and are under the age of sixty-five. They receive additional training before they begin working within a school.

* * *

The American educational system has evolved through its history to meet challenges, and there are many new challenges facing educators today. Issues like standardized testing and school choice remain areas of contention in debates about America's public school systems. While American education has made great progress, it is still significantly impacted by race, ethnicity, social class, gender, and other factors.

The importance of education is impossible to overstate, and perhaps this is why so many passionate debates emerge in discussing reform, standardized testing, curriculum standards, and other hot topics in education today.

TEXT-DEPENDENT QUESTIONS

1. Who was Horace Mann?
2. What landmark Supreme Court case ended the legal segregation of American schools?
3. What was the effect of the 1975 Education for All Handicapped Children Act (EAHCA)?

 RESEARCH PROJECTS

Discrimination is a significant issue in schools today and in the past. Choose a group to research. Examples include Asian female students or male students from families of low socioeconomic status. Find five statistics about this group and create a presentation in which you discuss these statistics and the potential factors leading up to them.

**achievement gap**—the disparity in performance between different groups of students in grades, test scores, and drop-out rates.

**advocates**—those who publicly support or recommend something.

**Montessori**—a method of teaching that involves allowing children to develop natural interests, foregoing formal teaching.

**quantify**—to measure or determine somthing.

# CAN THE EDUCATION SYSTEM BE REFORMED?

CHAPTER 2

Education reform **advocates** want to change the current system of public education, usually to focus on improving student achievement. Pro-reform organizations believe that improvements to the education system will lead to large returns in national wealth, well-being, and health.

Some of the reforms that have been championed in the past have included changing the length of the school day or the duration of the school year, offering after-school tutoring programs, lowering class sizes, and creating charter schools as alternatives to failing public schools.

Most reform proposals have had mixed results, at best, when they have been implemented. Attempts to **quantify** teaching results so that teachers and administrators can be held accountable have resulted in numerous scandals, as schools try to cover up poor performances on tests so that they will meet the benchmarks they need to continue receiving federal and state funding. Opponents of reform point out that despite the improvement in high school graduation rates, many studies indicate that American student achievement does not compare favorably with students from other developed nations. They argue that, so far, the results of school reforms have been illusory.

In the following essays, you will read opposing viewpoints regarding the ability of the United States to reform its current education system.

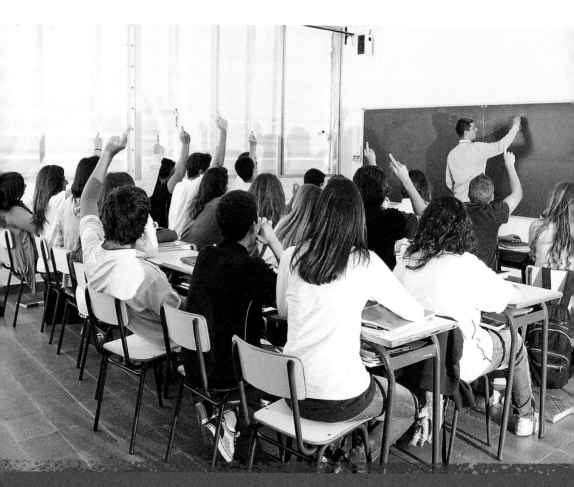

*A recent study highlighted the difficulty in retaining good young teachers. It found that 14 percent of new teachers resign by the end of their first year, and almost 50 percent leave within five years.*

# THE EDUCATION SYSTEM CAN BE REFORMED

Reforming the nation's education system is not only necessary; it's possible. By focusing on areas in which schools are currently lacking, the nation's public education system can change for the better. Evidence suggests that change is on the horizon.

One of the best ways to reform the education system is to make teachers more effective by offering additional training. First, the school system must consider the characteristics it deems important for educators to possess. Creating a common standard for teachers to achieve could lead to more effective education. Some experts believe that the creation of Common Core is a step in the right direction.

Next, instruction programs for educators should become not only more rigorous, but also more selective. It should be more difficult to become a teacher, and training programs could focus admitting only the best prospective educators.

Accountability for teachers is crucial, and must extend beyond rating how well classes perform on standardized tests. Accountability should begin with teaching education programs that provide rigorous academic standards. Teacher education should include coursework that helps teachers to fulfill school district needs.

Additionally, school districts should be encouraged to hire and retain the teachers who are most qualified. Too often, districts allow financial considerations to get in the way of this. Teachers with many

*"The purpose of school should not be to prepare students for more school. We should be seeking to have fully engaged students now."[5]*
*—Donalyn Miller, educator*

years of experience are often given incentives to retire early, so that the district can save money by hiring recent graduates at the lower levels of the salary guide. The most highly qualified educators have often taken additional coursework related to teaching. When school districts change their recruiting practices, they may see drastic changes in the quality of teachers in schools.

High turnover rates for teachers are common in the worst performing school districts. "Attracting and maintaining a stable faculty of qualified teachers at schools serving many low-income, low-performing, and minority students is particularly difficult, even when incentives are available," notes the National Academy of Education. "Financial incentives such as bonuses may attract teachers initially, but many quickly move on when their obligation is over. We need to find the financial and other incentives that will induce good teachers to stay in schools where they are most needed."[6]

Teachers working in low-performing schools often must do more work than their counterparts working in high-performing schools, and they are often paid less. Teachers in low-performing institutions often lack educational resources and work alongside colleagues who are often not as qualified as those at more prestigious schools. This must change in order to benefit students and teachers.

*To see Bill Gates discuss education reform, scan here.*

So, what incentives can schools and districts offer to decrease turnover rates? Loan forgiveness and tuition reimbursements are two possible ways to sweeten the deal for teachers asked to work in positions deemed undesirable. Some districts are offering relocation and housing cost assistance as well.

Of course, not all incentives to get teachers to stay are financial. Some teachers simply ask for better support when they start a new job. Mentoring and coaching in the early years of teaching can help build a sense of community among those who might otherwise feel lost in the shuffle. Emotional and occupational support are crucial for helping new teachers feel comfortable at work.

Teachers also ask for better working conditions overall. About one-quarter of teachers who quit their jobs in one 2016 study reportedly had problems with assessment and accountability procedures. "Teaching conditions—which also define learning conditions for students—are a strong predictor of teachers' decisions about where to teach and whether to stay," noted the study's authors. "Working conditions are often much worse in high-poverty than in low-poverty schools and contribute to high rates of teacher turnover in these schools."[7]

Mandated curriculum and standardized testing also contributed to the decision to quit, with some teachers complaining that school districts are putting too much emphasis on test scores, rather than education.

Additionally, the education system should focus on

improving the roles of individuals in leadership positions, like superintendents and principals. Principals who micromanage their teachers may find it difficult to keep track of the greater learning community. Some schools have found success by reshuffling district priorities, reducing the number of schools supervisors were in charge of, and providing support rather than simply enforcing compliance.[8]

*Teachers report feeling "burned out" because their work is stressful, and they feel that they are not supported or respected.*

Increasing opportunity for professional development for principals may facilitate these changes.

Of course, reform is also about student needs. Reform also involves focusing on the most effective ways for students to learn. While many classrooms favor lecture styles,

##  REDUCING CLASS SIZES

One common proposal for education reform is to reduce class sizes in schools. Research suggests that smaller class sizes can be beneficial for students in many ways. For example, students in small classes who require extra instruction may receive more individualized attention. Teachers also have an opportunity to create customized instruction plans based on the needs of their smaller groups. Small class sizes also provide opportunities for more hands-on activities, and teachers in these classrooms can provide greater feedback for each student.

There have been efforts to legislate smaller class sizes. Nationally, the ratio of students to teachers in public schools has fallen from 17.6 students per teacher in 1980 to 16.1 students per teacher in 2014. However, this figure also counts special education classes, as well as other specialized courses

active and cooperative learning techniques allow more room to develop. Active learning involves an emphasis on giving students a way to participate rather than to simply listen. Cooperative learning often involves group and team work. Those who promote child-centered learning, like proponents of Montessori schools, might claim that reform in this area is possible.

Reforming the system should also include a focus on the achievement gap in the nation's schools. When re-

that typically have fewer students enrolled. The US Department of Education reports that the average size of most regular education classrooms is around 25 students per teacher.

While lower class sizes can be worthwhile educationally, many districts find that they cannot afford the cost. An elementary school with forty-five students enrolled in third grade might normally have two classrooms of twenty-two or twenty-three students. If that school choses to divide the students among three classes of fifteen students, another teacher must be hired, and classroom space must be found or created. The new teachers may find themselves teaching in spaces originally intended to be administrative offices, or in trailers. As a result, smaller class sizes are not always an option, especially for school districts in low-income areas or that are facing budgetary concerns.

*Many American school buildings were constructed during the 1950s and 1960s. They often require expensive renovations to replace old pipes and inefficient systems, and create appropriate spaces for modern education.*

searchers talk about the achievement gap, they are talking about the difference in test scores and grades between minority students and student from lower socioeconomic backgrounds compared to other students. Factors like race, ethnicity, gender, first language, income, and disability all impact the achievement gap. Technology, child-focused reforms, and teacher-focused reforms can help lessen the gap.

Many of the issues reported in the nation's schools include dangerous conditions and necessary repairs. In Washington, D.C., some schools must wait for more than a year for urgent repairs. A 2014 report issued by the US Department of Education indicated that about half of all schools in the United States require repairs or some form of modernization.[9] Funding is a significant issue for schools in need of repairs, so adding funds to school budgets may pave the road for reforms.

Improving the environment in which students are expected to learn is critical. Many students attend institutions that are dangerous or in areas of high violent crime. Research demonstrates that most violent crimes committed by juveniles occur in the hours immediately following the end of the school day.[10] Many of the reforms that will better the school system will actually be those that begin with other parts of the community, including local police departments. Finding common ground where school districts and other community organizations can work together can create a more harmonious atmosphere for students.

Implementing these reforms will be a challenge. Making changes little by little is a key component in facilitating change. In spite of the challenges reform may pose, educators and students deserve to work in safe, effective environments.

# EDUCATION REFORMS HAVE NOT WORKED

In 2007, the public schools in Washington, D.C., were failing, and the city government took over control of the schools from the school district. A decade later, the capital's schools were being praised by educational experts as models of successful reform, with high graduation rates and test scores. Unfortunately, the improvements credited to school reform turned out to be largely a mirage. An investigation found that up to one-third of the district's 2017 graduates should not have been eligible to receive diplomas. School administrators, it turned out, had covered up excessive absences by students, faked test scores, and promoted some students from grade to grade regardless of their actual performance in the classroom, just so that the district would look good on paper.

Washington, D.C., is not the only school district to experience scandals related to educational reform programs that have not worked as originally intended. Other districts have experienced some of the same problems. Ultimately, it seems there are many barriers to meaningful reform of America's education system. These barriers are not conducive to reforming the school system, no matter how much the districts, students, and teachers could benefit from them. Even with collaborative measures, school districts across the nation typically fail to follow through when proposed reforms don't deliver the promised results.

Bureaucratic stagnation makes it very difficult for schools and districts to implement incentives that lead

*In 2017, investigators found that the Washington, D.C., public school system had inflated its graduation rates by passing students who should not have been eligible for diplomas. This was done so that the school would meet certain benchmarks established by the federal government to qualify for federal education funding.*

to reform. Any time change is proposed—whether it is at the school district level, or in local or state government, existing bureaucracies often place roadblocks in the path. Even people who have good ideas are often unable to effect meaningful changes.

The power of teachers' unions affects the nation's ability to reform schools. For example, labor agreements may impact a school district's ability to utilize merit pay

*"We stigmatize mistakes. And we're now running national education systems where mistakes are the worst thing you can make."*[4]
   *—Ken Robinson, author and education adviser*

and similar reforms. Schools do not have the final say in what they want to offer new and existing teachers; changes would have to be negotiated with the union and agreed to by both sides. Offering incentives to new teachers may anger long-time employees of the district who have been earning less money for years. Such a change could prompt the more experienced teachers to leave the district or school. Striking the right balance of payment for teachers, both old and new, can be difficult.

Another issue teachers face is that teachers' unions

typically require schools to value seniority more than performance. In 2011, Adam Gray was selected as the "Teacher of the Year" for the state of Massachusetts. A few weeks later, he was laid off by the school district, which had been forced to cut positions for budgetary reasons. In this case a highly talented teacher lost his job simply because he had not been at the school as long as other educators.[11] Tenure and seniority programs also make it difficult for school districts to assess teacher performance. If schools can't fire poor performing teachers now, how can they implement sweeping reforms?

This is not to blame the teachers. The truth is, teachers are often overworked and must use their own time and resources to keep the classroom going. Schools, districts, states, and even the federal government ask a lot of teachers, while also expecting these educators to continue delivering high scores on tests. Many teachers would be willing to help make improvements to the system, but reform must be a group effort.

Some people have argued that if schools were run more like businesses, a more efficient system could be developed. However, business owners can make personal decisions for the direction of their organizations that school administrators cannot.

Legal and political issues also create roadblocks for reform. Over the past three decades, presidents Clinton, Bush, and Obama all tried to reform education in the United States. These federal-level "reforms" have involved

Public school teachers on strike in downtown Chicago. Teachers'
unions fight for better pay and working conditions for their
members. However, they may make reforms harder to implement by
resisting proposed changes to tenure programs or the curriculum.

throwing taxpayer money at problems, rather than truly overhauling the educational system. In addition, each change in presidential leadership comes with new strategies for innovation and reform, which often counteract the programs a previous leader put in place. How can reform work when changes feel so constant?

The nation also struggles with a lack of interest on behalf of both parents and educators. School leaders must be motivated to make changes in the system, and parents are often too busy to invest time and energy in their children's education. Additionally, parents may not recognize the need for reforms, especially if they have not worked in the school system or gone to school in many years. With so many parents needing to work, they simply do not have the ability to spend much time in the classroom.

One of the biggest barriers to reform is the financial burden making such changes would incur. For instance, repairing and modernizing schools throughout the United States would cost nearly $200 billion, according to the National Center for Education Statistics. "53 percent of public schools needed to spend money on repairs, renovations, and modernizations to put the school's onsite buildings in good overall condition," noted the report. "The total amount needed was estimated to be approximately $197 billion, and the average dollar amount for schools needing to spend money was about $4.5 million per school."[12]

Along the same lines, some schools simply cannot afford to hire new full-time teachers. An article in *NEA*

*Today*, a publication of the National Education Association, drew attention to a school in Oakland that hired substitute teachers each day for an eighth grade math class because the district could not afford to hire a full-time teacher. "They live in a high-poverty neighborhood where school funding is so low the district finds it cheaper to hire a series of substitutes rather than pay a full-time teacher," reported Cindy Long. "As a result, the eighth graders don't have access to a high quality teacher, or the chance to learn very much math."[13] School districts that serve poor neighborhoods where minority students live  are more likely to have situations like these. If such schools cannot afford to pay qualified teachers, how could funds be allocated to make meaningful reforms?

Education reform would be beneficial, but any reforms would be complex, costly, and time-consuming. Unfortunately, under the current system it seems impractical to create the conditions where meaningful reforms can be implemented.

## TEXT-DEPENDENT QUESTIONS

1. What barriers exist for teachers who want to see reforms in education?
2. Which groups are linked to gaps in education and achievement?
3. What are some benefits of smaller class sizes?

 ## RESEARCH PROJECTS

Choose one proposed reform for education, like improved teacher training or smaller class size. What are the pros and cons of this specific type of reform? What barriers exist to this reform coming to fruition? Has any school, district, or state been able to utilize this kind of reform? What were the results?

## WORDS TO UNDERSTAND

**transparency**—clarity or translucency. Something that is transparent is clear or unsecretive.

**onus**—duty or responsibility.

**remedial**—addressing issues with learning. Remedial classes allow students to catch up.

# IS COMMON CORE CURRICULUM EFFECTIVE?

# CHAPTER 3

Common Core is the name for a set of academic standards in mathematics and English language arts/literacy. The Common Core standards outline what a student should know or be able to do as they complete each grade. The standards were put into place after calls to make high school students better prepared for college and the workplace. Although the federal government encourages states to adopt the Common Core standards, states are not required to do so.

Under Common Core, standards for reading increase in complexity at each grade level, creating progressive development in reading comprehension. Teachers are encouraged to promote both classic and contemporary authors, including Nathaniel Hawthorne, William Shakespeare, and Amy Tan. At the same time, Common Core encourages states and school districts to create more detailed reading lists. Students will read texts, ranging from entire books to short passages, after which they are expected to answer questions to demonstrate reading comprehension skills.

Writing is another staple of Common Core. Writing skills progress with each grade level. For example, kindergarten students learn to dictate stories to adults, whereas seniors in high school develop claims and counterclaims as part of a long essay. Students are expected to graduate with the ability to write logically, supporting their opinions, and to be able to complete research projects of varying lengths.

Speaking and listening skills are part of Common Core as well. Students must be able to participate in one-on-one discussions, in small groups, and in whole-class activities. Students also participate in formal and informal presenta-

## IMPLEMENTATION OF COMMON CORE

Since Common Core was first introduced in 2010, forty-seven states and the District of Columbia have chosen to adopt the standards. Only Alaska, Nebraska, Texas, and Virginia did not join the Common Core program. Each of these states instead developed their own educational standards.

Over the years, a number of other states have formally withdrawn from Common Core. In 2013, for example, Alabama opted out of Common Core standards. The state's governor, Robert Bentley, argued at the time that Common Core represented an intrusion by the federal government on his state's right to choose its school curriculum. Several other states, including Florida, Indiana, and South Carolina,

tions and discussions. Additionally, students are expected to lead their own discussions.

Common Core also encourages teaching of media and technology in the classroom. For example, students are expected to learn keyboarding skills. Controversially, Common Core does not include a standard for learning cursive writing, though many states (including California, Louisiana, and Tennessee) still require cursive to be taught. Critics of Common Core argue that being able to read cursive writing is important for those who need to read and interpret historical documents, and that being able to write in cursive allows students to communicate quickly and clearly.

have also withdrawn from Common Core. Each of these states subsequently implemented their own "college and career ready" standards that are, for the most part, in line with Common Core.

A few states have adopted part of the standards. Delaware, for example, incorporated elements of both the ELA and math standards into its state curriculum. Minnesota adopted the English standards from Common Core, but developed its own standards for mathematics.

Although the state of Alaska did not adopt Common Core, the state does allow individual school districts to opt into the program. Alaska also allows parents to opt out of standardized testing if they do not want their children to participate.

Mathematics is another area of Common Core that is somewhat controversial. Not only does Common Core require students to solve problems, it also requires them to understand problem-solving techniques through abstract and quantitative reasoning. Different math standards are required for each grade level. The goal is for students to leave high school knowledgeable in geometry, statistics, number systems, and more.

Many people ask how Common Core has changed American education. The truth is that Common Core influences some specific ways in which students learn. For example, they are required to cite academic sources in cases in which students might have previously referred to personal beliefs or experiences. This skill is deemed much more useful for college and critical thinking skills. Additionally, children are expected to read more non-fiction texts than most schools previously required.

Math also has some specific but noticeable changes. For instance, parents will see that their children are learning fewer topics per grade, but they are delving into these topics on a more in-depth level. Additionally, students must build a deeper understanding of these topics because math skills build on each other.

Controversy continues to surround the implementation of Common Core. Some critics of the program are against the idea of having the federal government promote educational standards throughout all of the states. Each of the US states is different, and they argue that local or state

*Scan here to learn more about the Common Core standards.*

governments know better than the federal government what state residents should be learning. Some people also have problems with the rigorous nature of the material students are supposed to learn. But perhaps the largest source of controversy surrounding Common Core is not the standards themselves, but the level of standardized testing involved. In an effort to ensure that students are meeting end-of-school-year benchmarks, assessments have become a significant part of student life. Many educators and parents feel these standardized tests take away valuable educational time, and result in educators who "teach to the test" rather than helping students develop important learning skills.

The following essays examine some of the opposing viewpoints related to the implementation of Common Core.

# COMMON CORE IS EFFECTIVE

Common Core offers an excellent set of standards for students, making it possible to close the achievement gap. Students who live in states that utilize Common Core are likely to reap its benefits in the coming years. This essay presents just a few of the reasons why Common Core is a successful endeavor for states that accept it.

First, Common Core does not have to be a one-size-fits-all solution, in spite of what opponents claim. This set of standards provide room for growth and customization. Additionally, teachers have the benefit of grading students based on their individual merits rather than on a curve. Teachers can track each student's progress throughout the year without the subjective nature of grades.

This set of standards does not impact every subject. For example, Common Core does not necessarily set standards for art, science, physical education, and social studies, though students will read some scientific and historical texts as part of literature studies. This lends way for creativity and innovation. States and school districts can make their own decisions for approaching these topics.

While Common Core presents some groundwork, educators can still present material creatively. In fact, some teachers say Common Core has allowed them to become more creative in the classroom. "I've been faced with the challenge of having to teach roughly 100 math topics over the course of a single year," one fourth-grade teacher told *NEA Today*. "The Common Core takes this smorgasbord of

> *"The standards are just that: standards, similar to those that have guided teachers in all states for years, except these standards are inspired by a simple and powerful idea: Every American student should leave high school with the knowledge and skills to succeed in college and in the job market."*[14]
>
> —Bill Gates,
> businessman and philanthropist

topics and removes things from the plate, allowing me to focus on key topics we know will form a clear and a consistent foundation for students."[16] By streamlining the content taught at each grade level, teachers can provide more detailed instruction, as well as more fun activities that enrich the learning experience.

Common Core provides readiness for life as an adult and higher education by increasing the rigor of classroom standards. This comes after many universities complained about the increased need for students to attend **remedial** courses. With previous sets of standards, students were not prepared for college. New assessments allow instructors to keep track of student progress to provide individual feedback to students falling short of targets. Frequent assessments may come with a negative connotation, but the truth is that they offer necessary feedback for parents and students.

The development of Common Core's English and language arts standards was based on the National Assessment of Educational Progress framework. This framework is based on public hearings, reviews by scholars, and involvement of supervisors. Common Core math standards come from the Trends in International Mathematics and Science Study, which compares the achievements and skills of American students to those in other countries. In using these two sources, Common Core facilitates learning to a level on par with students in other countries.

One of the most beneficial features of Common Core is that the results compare favorably to the standards of other developed countries. The math standards are better than many of the former state standards Common Core

*Common Core provides opportunities for students to work collaboratively.*

replaced. In fact, states do not have to lower their own standards at all. Increasing classroom rigor means students build higher expectations for themselves. While the United States may have been falling behind in math and language, Common Core seeks to raise the bar. When students have more to aspire to, they may try harder.

This set of standards also means that schools will eventually spend less money on test development, scoring, and reporting. These schools do not need to develop unique tests because the same assessments can be used throughout the nation. Once the initial costs of transitioning are complete, schools may see lower costs associated with it.

Additionally, unified standards allow states using Common Core to compare their tests scores against each other accurately. For example, schools in California can now compare their data to schools in Florida easily. This allows better decisions about the needs of each state when they can accurately compare student progress and achievement.

A side benefit of Common Core is that students graduating from high school may need to take fewer remedial classes. In 2016, one-quarter of all first-year college students needed remedial education to catch up. These courses did not count toward a degree and wound up costing students and parents $1.5 billion.[17] Common Core may reduce the number of remedial courses college students take.

Thanks to Common Core standards, students can no longer simply arrive at the correct answer. Educators can evaluate the critical thinking and problem-solving skills of their students when students must show their work. Teachers can use student work to see where problems in learning happen most often in the class. The critical thinking skills students learn as part of Common Core help them through adult life.

Common Core curriculum gives students a better understanding of why they are learning something. The standards set clear expectations. Additionally, parents and students can easily read the standards for themselves and understand what students are supposed to learn in the upcoming year. **Transparency** regarding school standards encourages parent participation.

Teachers also benefit from the use of Common Core curriculum, allowing them to work together to share resources. In meetings with other teachers, specific support is available. They can also attend targeted professional development events. Additionally, teachers will find the textbooks to be much more efficient for each subject and more specific for each grade level.

Finally, students who move from one school district or state to another will have a better chance of moving somewhere with standards similar to the place they moved from. Mobile students do not have to feel lost when they move to a new school in a new state.

Common Core is not a perfect solution, and it may not work in every situation. The good news is that teachers can adjust teaching methods to ensure they can reach out to each student effectively.

# COMMON CORE IS NOT EFFECTIVE

Common Core may appear to have established higher standards for learning, but unfortunately this set of standards does not hit the right marks. Everyone should be able to support improved critical thinking, better communication skills, and making students "college and career ready." But the reality is that Common Core actually inhibits innovation and creativity among both students and teachers.

Common Core and similar programs have resulted in an increasing reliance on standardized tests to determine which schools are succeeding and which are failing. As a result, teachers often feel compelled to narrow their focus so that their students will perform well on the standardized tests. They wind up dismissing some of the more creative aspects of teaching—the sorts of things that studies show foster true learning and create a lifelong love of knowledge. Teachers are no longer trusted to bring innovative lessons to the classroom, and it shows.

"Academic creativity has been drained from degraded and overworked experienced teachers. Uniformity has sucked the life out of teaching and learning," writes David Greene in *US News and World Report*. "Good and great teachers leave and are replaced by new and cheap workers more willing to follow fool-proof, factory-like, prescribed lesson plans. In fact, the average teaching tenure has dropped from approximately 15 years of service in 1990 to less than five in 2013."[18]

A common complaint is that educators are "teaching

*"The debate needs to be broader. It needs to be about real accountability, school choice, high standards. If people don't like Common Core, fine. Just make sure your standards are much higher than the ones you had before. We can't keep dumbing down standards."*[15]
—*Jeb Bush, former governor of Florida*

to the test." Students must focus on performance and accountability, often to a level that is inappropriate for their age group. Test prep takes up too much classroom time that could be used to focus on more creative endeavors. Teachers spend a significant portion of time showing students how to answer test questions about vocabulary and comprehension rather than actually reading works of fiction that would help them build a knowledge base from which they could draw from.

In an effort to comply with Common Core standards, some schools have been forced to reduce the quality of the education they offer in order to appease the standards. In an effort to teach math in a way required by state curriculum guidelines, students may miss out on other helpful math lessons that might be more applicable to adult life.

In addition, the focus on Common Core takes time and resources away from art, music, STEM programs, and other related subjects. In fact, school districts could completely eliminate their arts programs and this would not impact their school ratings, which are based on meeting the Common Core benchmarks. However, educators agree that the arts are extremely valuable, giving young people skills to navigate an unpredictable world and assisting the development of creative and critical thinking.

Another disadvantage is the idea that Common Core assumes each high school student will go on to college. The Bureau of Labor Statistics found that just under 70 percent of high school students who graduated in 2016 went on to college.[19] Under Common Core, every student follows the same curriculum for their academic subjects, rather than tracking the college-bound students into college prep or advanced placement (AP) courses that will prepare them for college. This results in the high numbers of students who must take remedial courses once they get to college. It would better to place the **onus** on colleges to accept students who are prepared to handle the coursework they would find in the university.

Implementing the Common Core standards can provide a difficult transition for teachers and students. One reason for this is that the standards may seem vague. Teachers are still in the trenches trying to figure out Common Core and how to best implement the standards in the classroom. Until teachers have a better idea of what will be on the assessments students take, they may struggle to meet student needs.

Common Core resources, like new textbooks, are expensive. The fact that assessments are conducted online also means increased costs on technology simply for evaluations. California's 2015 budget originally included a $3.5 billion reimbursement specifically for public schools to cover the costs associated with Common Core. The actual costs associated with Common Core for the state,

*Opponents of Common Core complain that implementation will cost taxpayers a lot of money while not significantly improving education.*

when factoring in the increased technology costs, actually totaled more than $10 billion. This is just the tip of the iceberg. The nation's spending to implement Common Core exceeds $80 billion. "Since California, like the federal government and many state governments, faces a crushing debt crisis, future generations will have to pay twice for Common Core: once in stunted math abilities and again in taxes those stunted abilities will make harder to earn," writes Joy Pullmann.[20]

Another disadvantage of Common Core is the lack of equivalency for students with special needs. Special education teachers are forced to implement the Common Core curriculum in their classrooms, no matter where the students stand in their own skills and abilities. The standards and rules for assessment that go with them seem to ignore the needs of students with cognitive disabilities. Specific criteria, like those requiring students to be able to make predictions or assess character personality, may become a bigger struggle for individuals with autism, for example.

"Forcing all students into the same, age-pegged standards deprives atypical students of optimized learning opportunities and attainable goals at their level of developmental readiness," explains special education teacher Katherine Beale in *The Atlantic*. "Far better ... for a student with autism to engage with simplified social scenarios that he can work through on his own than to muddle through complex ones that need to be explained to him piecemeal. As any of my special-ed student teachers can tell you, and as research has shown, restricting students to curricula beyond their cognitive capacities substantially lowers their achievement. The purported goal of the Common Core is success for all students. But success for all requires openness towards cognitive diversity, and isn't so easily standardized."[21]

In addition, Common Core takes away some aspects of school choice. Parents once had the ability to move their children to a different school or classroom if they had an objection to the curriculum or methods of teaching. When all schools are following the same curriculum, parents may have a more difficult time finding a school that they feel will meet their child's needs.

Finally, Common Core neglects the local context of an area. Students living in rural Texas may have a different cultural context to draw from than students living in New York City. Students living on a reservation in Arizona may have different experiences than students living in Hawaii. In order for assessments to truly measure skills and abilities, test writers must acknowledge potential cultural bias and ensure every student has the same opportunity to be successful.

There are positive aspects to Common Core, but as currently implemented the program certainly has downsides. Instead of focusing on student individuality, Common Core ultimately is about ensuring that students conform to the same skill sets and abilities. Whether or not this is a realistic, or desirable, goal remains to be seen.

## TEXT-DEPENDENT QUESTIONS

1. When was Common Core introduced into class-rooms?
2. How much did Common Core cost to implement up to this point?
3. What subjects do Common Core standards cover?
4. What is one reason schools decided to use Common Core?

 ## RESEARCH PROJECTS

Read the Common Core standards (available at http://www.corestandards.org/read-the-standards/). First, choose a subject (language or math). Then, select a grade level you have completed. Look at the list of standards for that subject and level and choose one specific standard. Write a one-page essay in which you discuss the ways in which you became successful in achieving this standard.

## WORDS TO UNDERSTAND

**charter**—a written document by some power granting an institution, like a school, some rights and responsibilities.

**discipline**—a branch of knowledge, typically one studied in higher education.

**education management organization**—a for-profit company that manages elementary or secondary schools. These companies have been criticized by educators as being profit-centered, rather than student centered.

**mandated**—something that is required or commanded.

# DO CHARTER SCHOOLS BENEFIT STUDENTS?

# CHAPTER 4

Over the past few decades, "school choice" has emerged as an important issue among parents who are looking for the best options for their children's education. In some areas, particularly low-income neighborhoods, public school systems may fail to deliver a high-quality education to students. This could be because the school is poorly managed, or because of the school district's general lack of resources. In recent years, parents whose public school systems are failing have turned to charter schools, hoping to find a place where their children can succeed as students in a safe environment.

Charter schools are a new type of public school. The state government grants a **charter** to an organization that is formed to operate the school. Some charter schools are run by government agencies or universities; others by community members who create nonprofit organizations to run the schools. A few states—including Arizona, Michigan, and Wisconsin—allow charter schools to be managed by for-profit **education management organizations**, although this is controversial in educational circles.

Charter schools are independent from oversight by

the local district's elected board of education, and do not have to follow the same rules as other public schools in the district. At the same time, they are required to meet more stringent accountability benchmarks in exchange for this sense of educational freedom. Each state sets limits on how many charter schools may exist within a particular school district or municipal area.

Charter schools are not the same as private schools. They are supported by tax revenue, and are free to those who are admitted. Regular public schools are usually supported by local property taxes, but charter schools receive payments from state governments, often on a per-pupil basis. Rather than having a general curriculum like other public schools, charter schools often focus on a particular **discipline**. Some charter schools emphasize math, science, or engineering. Others might focus on music or the arts.

A regular public school must admit any student that lives within its district borders. Charter schools require prospective students to apply for admission, although there are no exams or specific requirements to attend. Often, more students apply to charter schools than there are spaces available. When this happens, the school will select students for the open slots through a lottery, with those who are not selected going onto a waiting list.

"Charter schools have evolved to have many distinctive features," writes Karl Zinsmeister in *Philanthropy* magazine. "They generally have longer school days and longer school years. Many place high expectations on students

> *"Charter schools are public schools that operate, to a certain extent, outside the system. They have more control over their teachers, curriculum, and resources. They also have less money than public schools."*[22]
> *—Maggie Gallagher, educator*

(resulting in 100 percent college acceptance at many leading inner-city charters). They often have strict discipline, and many require parents and students to sign contracts that commit them to serious duties. Many recruit teachers and principals outside of traditional credential channels, seeking particularly creative and dedicated individuals. Charters have been extremely innovative in shaping teacher pay, creating curricula, experimenting with class structures, and adapting technology. They often share a commitment to rigorous testing and sharing student results with parents and the public."[24]

Today, the United States has more than 6,900 charter schools, which educate more than three million students.

They tend to receive less funding than regular public schools; recent studies indicate that charter schools get about 80 percent of the funding that public schools receive. The charter schools make up the difference through fundraising and philanthropic donations.

Charter schools can, and do, close down due to low enrollment, lack of funding, or poor performance that results in a failure to meet the requirements established in their charter. It is estimated that about one-third of charter schools close before they are ten years old. However, hundreds of new charter schools are opened each year throughout the United States.

The following essays discuss some of the benefits and drawbacks to charter schools. Because the laws that govern charter schools vary from state to state, there are many different perspectives regarding their efficacy.

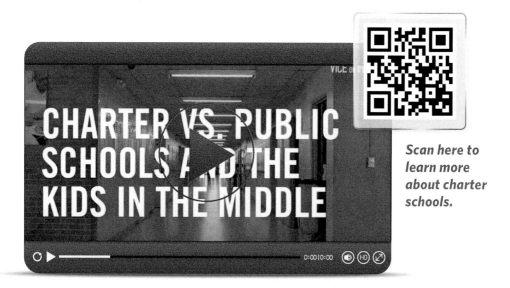

*Scan here to learn more about charter schools.*

# CHARTER SCHOOLS BENEFIT STUDENTS

One of the best reforms in our country's education system has been the addition of charter schools. Students who attend charter schools reap their benefits, and students who want to attend public schools are free to pursue this avenue as well. School choice is a crucial part of providing children with solid educational options.

One of the biggest benefits of charter schools is the smaller class sizes, which can give public school students a private school experience. Students who are introverted or shy may benefit from being in smaller classes that make it easier to speak up. Small class sizes also benefit students who prefer a closer relationship to a teacher. Finally, studies indicate that smaller class sizes are better for preventing bullying among students.

Teachers who work in charter schools are not required to adjust their teaching standards for standardized tests. At the same time, educators are still accountable to their sponsors, which could be a state agency, university, or local school board. School performance is measured because charters have to be renewed regularly, and subpar schools will not be renewed.

Additionally, students have the option for more customized learning options. If a student is struggling in one particular area, teachers can make quick changes on their own to address them. These quick changes are possible thanks to the lack of bureaucracy involved in charter school decisions.

In some cases, students even have the option of attending school online. Students who move a lot or who travel often will benefit from attending a virtual school. Plus, students may be able to pick between several online schools available to them.

Of course, on-campus learning is the more popular choice for charter school students. Students have the opportunity to attend a school that focuses solely on meeting their needs. For example, students who are interested in theater may opt to attend a charter school with a fantastic

 ## CYBER CHARTER SCHOOLS

Some of the newest charter schools are actually online, meaning students do not need to leave the house to gain an education.

Virtual charter schools offer much more flexibility for students. Those who are mobile or travel a lot with their family can still attend school without interruption. Additionally, this option allows parents to be active participants in their child's education. Students can also participate in other activities and events while going to school at any point throughout the day.

For children who are already ahead of the pace, online education may seem appealing. They can

performing arts program. Students who are interested in fitness might seek out a charter school that offers physical education as a priority. Charter schools that focus on technology and computer skills are also common.

Charter schools do not discriminate against students. Students of any race, religious affiliation, or income level attend charter schools. For many parents, the main conflict comes down to choosing between private schooling and charter schooling. Charter schooling offers the advantage of being free and not discriminatory. Private schools are not required to accept any particular student, whereas charter schools cannot pick and choose between the students. Applications are used only in the case that there is

participate in more individualized programs rather than waiting for the rest of the class to catch up.

However, some studies have shown that online school students tend to have lower reading and math skills than those educated in traditional schools. A recent study of one cyber charter school demonstrated that a majority of students were behind in math by a full grade level.[25] Additionally, half of all students were behind in reading. Many online charter-school students are unprepared for the challenges of college, too.

Ongoing investigations into virtual charter schools continue with the hope of addressing whether or not these schools can maintain their charter school status.

not enough room for every student in the school.

In fact, charter schools have the potential to offer more diversity than public schools. While public schools are typically composed of individuals in the neighboring community, a charter school can consist of individuals from any of the communities nearby.

Some people have concerns about the performance of racial minorities in charter schools. More black students in California charter schools met or exceeded standards than black students in public schools.[26] Studies also demonstrated that students living in poverty benefitted from charter schools.

Parents may appreciate the level of interaction they can have with charter schools. Parents have a real voice in a charter school, and facilities that do not make parents happy see a decrease in attendance and funding. Parents often feel they have more of a voice in these schools than in public institutions.

While charter schools do receive government funding, they sometimes seek additional funding elsewhere. Businesses and individuals are often willing to donate to charter schools. Receiving funding for school activities and events is not as difficult as many people believe.

Charter schools may very well be the future of education for American students. If the benefits of charter schools continue to increase with each upcoming year, students can not only succeed but also excel in college and career.

# CHARTER SCHOOLS DO NOT BENEFIT STUDENTS

Charter schools may benefit some students, but they may not offer the ideal circumstances for the current educational system. Not only can charter schools become a detriment to students who attend them, but they might also have an impact on the students attending public schools and the school system in general.

First, charter schools require increased fundraising, sometimes calling on students and parents to use more resources than other public schools. While charter schools do earn a rate per pupil, this rate is often much lower than for traditional public schools. On average, charter school budgets were nearly 20 percent less per pupil than public schools.[27] These schools struggle to find financing, meaning some students will end up learning in modular classrooms rather than in a permanent school. In the meantime, students, parents, and teachers may be working after hours to meet financial goals.

Additionally, charter schools have a problem with accountability. In six states, charter school authorizers were not required to view student progress. Another state body was required to review performance, which means the organization issuing the charter could be left in the dark regarding performance. How long could schools continue to operate without the charter authorizer knowing there is a problem?

Just because charter schools have their own standards and curriculum does not mean students will avoid taking state-**mandated** tests. If a student has test anxiety or hopes to avoid taking standardized testing altogether, attending a charter school is not a way to avoid them. Students at charter schools still take federally mandated testing unless they live in a state that allows them to opt out.

Charter schools also offer fewer extracurricular activities, including sports. In some cases, students at charter schools are allowed to go to public schools for extracurricular activities. Students often need these activities to broaden their social and physical horizons, especially if they are trying to make their profiles look desirable for universities. While some charter schools may offer sports and clubs, they tend to be smaller than those at public schools.

Additionally, charter schools may not necessarily work with disabled students or individuals with special needs. A charter school may require that parents pay to bring in their own assistants, though some parents might argue this is in opposition of IDEA, which serves to protect students with special education needs. The truth is that many charter schools lack the resources necessary to address specific special education needs.

Lack of socioeconomic diversity is a serious concern for students attending charter schools. Attempts to be more inclusive have included designations for weighted lotteries to be more inclusive of individuals living with economic disadvantages. These are the students who might otherwise not come to a charter school because they do not have transportation to different parts of town, for example.

*Milburn Schools was an education management organization that operated charter schools in Florida, Texas, and Washington, DC. Several of the Milburn schools were closed for failing to meet academic standards.*

Not only is diversity an issue, but charter schools in some states do participate in selective admissions. This can allow for discrimination because the admissions process could involve an interview with the family ahead of time. A charter school administrator could decide the child is not a good fit for the school for any reason they deem fit.

The lack of oversight over charter schools could lead to corruption. Corruption also comes into play considering the potential of for-profit schools. While many states have banned for-profit charter schools, others welcome them with open arms. Already, big names, including Bill and Melinda Gates, have invested billions of dollars into char-

*"Charters are an important option for parents in communities with failing schools and provide education laboratories. On average, charters are half the cost of public schools. They are an important component of our system and we continue to encourage their development on this budget."*[23]

—*Andrew Cuomo, governor of New York*

ter school education. Additionally, some people fear that privatized or for-profit education will ultimately try to take over public options.

In the same vein, some people might argue that the nature of charters schools has become politicized. Originally, charter schools were meant to eliminate bureaucracy and allow for more freedom. Some argue that now charter schools privatize education and have become a method of attacking teachers' unions.

Schools that fail to meet their set standards means institutions can be closed at any time for failure to meet them. When a charter school closes down, thousands of students can be left with no school to attend. That also leaves teachers out in the cold, searching for new jobs.

Keep in mind that teachers at charter schools may not have the same qualifications as teachers at public schools. States like Alabama, Louisiana, Mississippi, and Oklahoma do not require the same teacher certification as public schools in the states.[28] Some other states require only some of the staff members at charter schools to be certified.

One study demonstrated that charter school teachers are more likely to stop teaching than other public school

*In some communities, charter schools are formed to focus on a particular discipline, such as math, science, engineering, music, or the arts.*

educators. This could be related to the lack of teachers' unions and grueling hours charter school teachers are expected to put in at work.

Some types of charter schools are more commonly associated with the trend of teacher burnout. Charter facilities run by for-profit and nonprofit management groups rather than educational organizations are more likely to have a higher teacher turnover.[29] Studies suggest that the rate of teachers leaving the profession altogether increases in these charter schools. Reasons for leaving have included poor administrative support, few opportunities for professional development, low salary, and long hours. Teachers leaving is a shame for students, especially considering that the new teachers replacing their more experienced former educators are often inexperienced.

Finally, keep in mind that many charter schools have long wait lists. Students may have to attend a regular public school while awaiting enrollment, forcing them to switch schools in the middle of the year. A disruption in the student's school year can have social and academic consequences that one might eliminate by keeping the student at one school.

Charter schools ultimately present some benefits for students, but the model is not sustainable in the long run. With so many problems present in these early years of charter schools, public schooling options are the better choice for most children.

# TEXT-DEPENDENT QUESTIONS

1. When and where did charter schools first open?
2. Name one state that no longer allows for-profit charter schools.
3. Recall one pro and one con associated with online charter schooling.

 # RESEARCH PROJECTS

Identify one charter school in your city or state. When was the school founded? What are the school's goals? What is the application process for this school like? If you were a parent looking to make a choice for your child's education, would you consider this charter school. Write a paper discussing why or why not.

## WORDS TO UNDERSTAND

**standardized**—systemized or consistent.

**inequity**—lack of fairness.

**bias**—prejudice in favor of or against a person or group.

# IS STANDARDIZED TESTING RUINING EDUCATION?

# CHAPTER 5

Academic performance can tell a lot about the quality of a school's educational programs. **Standardized** testing is used to assess how effective educators are, as well as which schools are performing below or above expectations. The results of standardized tests can lead to incentives for some schools and consequences for others.

Standardized testing has been part of education since the late 1800s. However, since passage of the No Child Left Behind Act in 2002, educators have been required to place greater emphasis on standardized testing. NCLB was passed at a time that American students seemed to be falling behind students from other countries. The legislation required that school districts test students in third through eighth grades, as well as as in high school, to make sure that they were proficient in math and reading. The tests contributed to a school's ranking of Adequate Yearly Progress (AYP). Schools that were deemed not to meet the standard could lose federal funding or face corrective actions imposed by the state or federal Department of Education.

In December 2015, Congress passed the Every Student Succeeds Act (ESSA) to replace No Child Left Behind. ESSA requires that all students in the United States be taught to high academic standards that will prepare them to succeed in college and careers. The new legislation gave states more power to determine the standards that students are held to, and the outcomes that are measured by standardized tests. ESSA also included an emphasis on attendance and school graduation rates.

As always, there are two sides to the issue here. Some Americans feel standardized tests are fair for everyone and that the assessments are necessary and valuable. Opponents of standardized testing believe that testing takes away from a student's real education, that tests can be unintentionally **biased** to penalize some students, and that they fail to provide pertinent information that helps educators. Following are some of the arguments for and against standardized testing.

*Scan here to learn more about some student characteristics that standardized tests miss.*

# STANDARDIZED TESTING IS A PROBLEM

Many people have made valid complaints about the nature of standardized testing in the United States. While the premise of standardized testing seeks to understand more about student behavior, the truth is that testing poses many more problems than solutions.

One of the main complaints about standardized testing is the fact that it may inadvertantly incorporate cultural bias. Although educators agree that tests should not include cultural biases, they do still occur. Biased testing may include discussion of or allusion to cultural factors

*"Why have so many schools reduced the time and emphasis they place on art, music, and physical education? The answer is beyond simple: those areas aren't measured on the all-important tests. You know where those areas are measured . . . in life!"*[30]
*—Dave Burgess, author and public speaker*

a student may not be familiar with. Ultimately, culturally biased testing is **inequitable**, and does not make it equally possible for all students to succeed.

An example of culturally biased testing occurs in this test question: Which word is most similar to the word "cup"? The answer choices are, "Wall," "saucer," "table," or "window." A child who is not familiar with the word "saucer" may select the word "table" instead, because both are found in a kitchen.[32] Biased testing has prompted some students to simply give up on testing or even to boycott the tests in general.

*Students with physical handicaps or learning disabilities may be at a disadvantage when taking standardized tests.*

English-learners and students with special needs may perform poorly on these exams at no fault of their own. Students in special education programs fail to receive the services and accommodations they typically need during test-taking, prompting additional stress. One woman reported that the long testing sessions caused her son, who was in a wheelchair, to experience pressure sores and a respiratory infection.

Testing students in special education courses does not make sense, especially considering many students are separated from the mainstream curriculum. They often do not learn the same material as other students in the same level. Additionally, special education students may not receive the accommodations they often need to get through the testing. Even when accommodations are made, they are not always helpful. "Updated accommodations developed for Common Core tests like SBAC have not fulfilled their promise of giving [students with disabilities] better access to the tested material," notes a press release from the National Center for Fair and Open Testing. "For example, teachers described a dictation tool for SBAC testing that read the text rapidly in a robotic voice, leaving students baffled and unable to answer test questions."[33]

Additionally, standardized testing does not provide an accurate assessment of all the skills and abilities of a student. Even some colleges acknowledge this by accepting not only ACT or SAT scores but also by looking at the well-rounded nature of a student. Standardized testing in

*"But when I look back on the great teachers who shaped my life, what I remember isn't the way they prepared me to take a standardized test. What I remember is the way they taught me to believe in myself. To be curious about the world. To take charge of my own learning so that I could reach my full potential."[31]*

—*Barack Obama*

grades K-12 does not examine this additional information when determining the skills and abilities of younger students. A test cannot determine a child's social skills, ability to work well in a group, or creativity. Standardized testing misses a significant piece of the picture.

Previous studies have questioned whether standardized testing even present accurate findings that school administrators can use to make predictions or decisions. One study demonstrated that standardized testing fluctuations actually had a lot more to do with external factors rather than student performance.[34] Knowing this, it becomes much more difficult to justify using these tests to identify which schools are "good" and which are "bad."

Mandatory standardized testing often encourages educators to teach to the test, meaning students miss out on valuable curriculum. About 62 percent of teachers claimed they spent too much time in class preparing students to take state-required tests.[35] The same study found that students in schools with medium to high poverty levels were more likely to spend a significant amount of time on test preparation.

Teachers who are forced to spend so much time on test prep are losing morale, at least according to one study. Approximately 60 percent of those who participated in the study claimed they were losing enthusiasm for their

**"Half my students have Post Assessment Stress Disorder."**

job.[36] While the majority of teachers did claim they enjoy their school or school district, many teachers claimed they would seek employment in a different field if they could find a job that was financially feasible.

Placing undue importance on standardized tests also means that students are participating in assignments that do not encourage higher-level thinking. They are spending

 ## STANDARDIZED TESTING IN THE U.S.

Testing is by no means a new concept. Throughout history, people have been trying to find ways to compare and identify students whether it is to offer a job or to determine which students need the most intervention. During the nineteenth century, most school assessment was performed through oral recitations or through written essays. This differs very much from the method of standardized testing used today, which often consists of multiple-choice questions.

Throughout the late 1800s and early 1900s, researchers developed new methods of testing that would become much more useful with the growing student population. In 1890, colleges typically provided their own exams to judge which students

less time on complex assignments that challenge them to come up with unique ideas and more time learning tactics for taking multiple-choice exams.

Additionally, these tests typically examine only math and language skills. This means school curriculum shrinks lessons in science, social studies, art, and other fields. In one survey, 75 percent of teachers who claimed they were using fewer current events stories in class said they were doing so because they needed to focus on standardized testing topics.[37] As a result, students were focusing less on the world around them in the classroom.

would be eligible for admission to their schools. Harvard President Charles William Eliot changed this by suggesting all schools should rely on one exam. Within ten years, the College Entrance Examination Board was established.

Of course, education was not the only field in which standardized tests prevailed. During and after World War I, the military relied on testing results to determine which jobs people were eligible for.

Today's high school students will probably take more than a dozen standardized tests by the time they graduate. One of the best-known standardized tests is the SAT, which has been used by the College Board since 1926. The test encompasses language and math, and student scores often help them get into college.

In the same vein, these tests can actually place undue pressure and stress on students. Younger students are especially vulnerable to this test anxiety, which can have physical symptoms like crying and vomiting.[38] Children as young as eight feel the pressure to test well, prompting severe anxiety in some cases, especially after teachers have spent weeks discussing the significance of the testing. The pressure to succeed is in full force.

*Critics of standardized tests note that they do not provide feedback on how to perform better. Often, the teachers and students don't receive the results for several months.*

The pressure is not only on the students either. Teachers and schools are also under high demand to deliver results. In the past, this pressure has actually prompted some teachers to help students cheat or to change student answers. One case involved eleven Atlanta educators cheating. They were under strict pressure from administrators to show good results.[39] When something like this happens, the students suffer as well. They typically receive no score on the exam, and the educators are punished. Test score manipulation throws off all results.

All of this is not to mention that standardized testing is costly, and costs have been increasing in recent years. In 2012, standardized testing cost the nation $1.7 billion.[40] Pennsylvania alone spends $80 million for testing, not counting what individual schools and districts spend on test administration.[41] These figures leave the public wondering if testing students is worth the high cost.

Keeping all of this in mind, it is notable that the use of standardized tests has not improved student achievement as a whole. If anything, it would appear that teachers spend more time teaching students how to take tests. While No Child Left Behind was passed in an attempt to boost American performance on the world stage, the year after its implementation the country faced lower scores in math and science.

Standardized testing continues each year, impacting each new generation of students. Experimenting with these tests may harm students, not help them, in the long run.

# STANDARDIZED TESTING IS NOT A PROBLEM

While standardized testing may present some problems and roads for improvement, these exams are a crucial part of assessing the quality of education in the United States. For many reasons, the nation must continue the practice of testing and assessing American students.

First, standardized testing is a necessary metric for finding areas in which students, schools, and districts require improvement. Parents benefit from seeing their child's performance stacked against national standards. Without standardized tests, students may be forced to stay in low-performing schools without any governing body realizing the impact it has.

Additionally, other countries ranking highly on the national stage show benefits from using testing. China has been using standardized tests for centuries, and students there continue to demonstrate academic strengths. Shanghai has experienced especially high scores in recent years.[42] If American students are going to compete with students from other countries, assessments are a crucial component in gauging progress.

Understanding their child's achievement in academics also allows parents to make better choices for schooling. Standardized testing reports are sent to parents, allowing them to see where the school ranks against their student's performance. If a parent wants to send their child to a different school, they can do so with all the necessary knowledge in mind.

A 2013 study showed that for the most part, parents were happy with standardized testing. In fact, one of the biggest changes parents proposed was that performance on tests be used to make determinations against low-performing teachers. While this is an issue contested by teachers' unions, parents have showed support for testing. "I think the biggest crime is that teaching has turned to focus on

*Supporters of standardized testing say that they help educators to focus on the specific skills and basic knowledge that all students need to master.*

*Careful analysis of standardized test scores can be a useful way for school administrators to evaluate the effectiveness of teachers.*

the tests, rather than the tests being a tool that help you understand. All the teaching and learning is on the subject being tested," one parent told the Associated Press. "You have to ask how much you're straightjacketing the teachers."[43]

Some opponents of testing may claim that students experience shame resulting from low test scores. In fact, the test results are completely confidential. Even students do not have to know their own scores. Students will not be treated differently by educators or other students based on their performance on these tests.

Grading of standardized tests is completely objective. Because assessments are performed via machine, a person is not in charge of handing out grades based on personal bias. Students are given the same test questions, meaning they are not separated based on assumptions about a student's background or culture.

Standardized testing is ultimately beneficial. More than 90 percent of studies seem to show that this form of testing has a positive effect on student achievement as a whole. This figure comes from a study examining one hundred years of testing, allowing the study to create a full picture of testing.

One common complaint about standardized tests is that teachers are forced to "teach to the test." While this may originally sound inadequate, often "teaching to the test" merely implies focusing on the core subjects students need to understand to be successful. Teachers focus on language and math skills not only because they are on the standardized tests but also because they are the most important subjects students need to learn. Additionally, the majority of teachers in one study claimed they did not have to neglect their regular teaching abilities in order to prepare students for the test.[44]

In the midst of complaints that standardized testing is not focused on every school subject, opponents of testing may forget that state and district testing focus on these subjects. States may focus on social studies or science to see where students stand. These tests may be more catered to state standards and cultural connection.

Standardized tests are used outside of the K-12 educational system. In fact, doctors, lawyers, and real estate agents also take standardized tests to become licensed to work in their respective fields. If testing is not effective in the nation's education system, these professional industries would not trust testing either.

Colleges and universities also expect students to be more knowledgeable than they have been when they enter school. One study showed that 66 percent of professors said primary and secondary institutions did not have high standards for students, who were learning too little.[45] Colleges began to increase educational requirements, and students were often rising to the occasion. Without standardized testing, could the system have expected this to happen?

While stress about taking an important test is completely normal, students must learn to participate in spite of anxiety. Standardized testing is normal and expected in classrooms. One study demonstrated that 95 percent of students experienced manageable stress before tests.[46] With such a small percentage of students claiming they feel so anxious it prevents them from taking the tests, it is not reasonable to call off standardized testing altogether.

One of the significant arguments against standardized testing is the fact that students with special needs are required to take the same tests as other students in their grade level. While many students with special needs may struggle with the tests, not giving them the chance to participate would be discriminatory. While schools should be able to accommodate students by offering oral versions of the exam, testing these students is essential.

Finally, many opponents to standardized testing discuss the role of cheating on these exams. While cheating has been an issue in a few cases, it is not the norm. A few cases of test manipulation do not negate decades of progress in testing.

Essentially, taking away standardized testing as a valid measurement for student progress means that fewer people are held accountable. Students are not held accountable for their required learning, teachers are not held accountable for their work, and schools are not held accountable for the quality of the education they provide. Eliminating standardized testing means nobody is held responsible.

Instead of blaming standardized testing for education failures in the United States, making improvements to the curriculum and teaching quality would be more beneficial. As of now, standardized testing presents the best way for the nation to stay up to date with its performance on an international level while also determining which students need more assistance than they are currently receiving.

# TEXT-DEPENDENT QUESTIONS

1. When was the first SAT examination held?
2. What is one benefit of standardized testing?
3. What act did President Obama overhaul?
4. How much does Pennsylvania spend on standard-ized testing each year?

# RESEARCH PROJECTS

Find an example of standardized testing used in your area. It could be the SAT, a state-mandated test, or a district-related exam. Write a few paragraphs discussing the history of the test. How have the test results been beneficial to students, educators, and even the government? Do you think this test is more beneficial or detrimental?

**affidavit**—a sworn statement, in writing, that sets out a person's testimony.

**affirmative action programs**—programs that are intended to improve the educational or employment opportunities of members of minority groups and women.

**BCE and CE**—alternatives to the traditional Western designation of calendar eras, which used the birth of Jesus as a dividing line. BCE stands for "Before the Common Era," and is equivalent to BC ("Before Christ"). Dates labeled CE, or "Common Era," are equivalent to Anno Domini (AD, or "the Year of Our Lord").

**colony**—a country or region ruled by another country.

**democracy**—a country in which the people can vote to choose those who govern them.

**discrimination**—prejudiced outlook, action, or treatment, often in a negative way.

**detention center**—a place where people claiming asylum and refugee status are held while their case is investigated.

**ethnic cleansing**—an attempt to rid a country or region of a particular ethnic group. The term was first used to describe the attempt by Serb nationalists to rid Bosnia of Muslims.

**felony**—a serious crime; in the United States, a felony is any crime for which the punishment is more than one year in prison or the death penalty.

**fundamentalist**—beliefs based on a strict biblical or scriptural interpretation of religious law.

**median**—In statistics, the number that falls in the center of a group, meaning half the numbers are higher than the number and half are lower.

**minority**—a part of a population different from the majority in some characteristics and often subjected to differential treatment.

**paranoia**—a mental disorder characterized by the strong belief that the person is being unfairly persecuted.

**parole**—releasing someone sentenced to prison before the full sentence is served, granted for good behavior.

**plaintiff**—a person making a complaint in a legal case in civil court.

**pro bono**—a Latin phrase meaning "for the public good," referring to legal work undertaken without payment or at a reduced fee as a public service.

**racial profiling**—projecting the characteristics of a few people onto the entire population of a group; for example, when police officers stop people on suspicion of criminal activity solely because of their race.

**racism**—discrimination against a particular group of people based solely on their racial background.

**segregation**—the separation or isolation of a race, class, or group from others in society. This can include restricting areas in which members of the race, class, or group can live; placing barriers to social interaction; separate educational facilities; or other discriminatory means.

# FURTHER READING

Baker, Nicholson. *Substitute: Going to School with a Thousand Kids*. New York: Blue Rider Press, 2016.

Cuban, Larry. *Why Is It So Hard to Get Good Schools?* New York: Teachers College, Columbia University, 2003.

Goldstein, Dana. *The Teacher Wars*. New York: Anchor Books, 2014.

Kliebard, Herbert. *The Struggle for the American Curriculum*. New York: Routledge & Kegan Paul, 1987.

Kozol, Jonathan. *Savage Inequalities*. New York: Broadway Paperbacks, 1991.

Lemann, Nicholas. *The Big Test: The Secret History of the American Meritocracy*. New York: Farrar, Straus and Giroux, 1999.

Nuthall, Graham. *The Hidden Lives of Learners*. New Zealand: New Zealand Council for Educational Research, 2007.

Ravitch, Diane. *The Death and Life of the Great American School System: How Testing and Choice Are Undermining Education*. New York: Basic Books, 2010.

Roza, Marguerite. *Where Do School Funds Go?* Washington, DC: The Urban Institute Press, 2010.

Tough, Paul. *How Children Succeed*. New York: Houghton Mifflin Company, 2012.

Weber, Karl. *Waiting for Superman*. New York: Participant Media, 2010.

Whelan, Fenton. *Lessons Learned: How Good Policies Produce Better Schools*. London: F. Whelan, 2009.

Willingham, Daniel T. *Why Don't Students Like School?: A Cognitive Scientist Answers Questions About How the Mind Works and What It Means for the Classroom*. San Francisco: Jossey-Bass, 2009.

# INTERNET RESOURCES

https://nces.ed.gov/programs/stateprofiles/
This website allows you to search for statewide information about elementary and secondary education. Information is available regarding demographics, public libraries, and national assessment progress.

https://www.edweek.org/ew/section/multimedia/map-states-academic-standards-common-core-or.html
This resource displays the current standing of Common Core standards throughout the United States. It displays information for each state regarding the choice to rewrite or pass legislation against Common Core.

http://www.corestandards.org/read-the-standards/
This website allows you to read the Common Core standards for language and math in their entirety.

http://www.nea.org/home/20380.htm
This website offers research and studies regarding students who are at risk for achievement gaps.

https://www.stopbullying.gov/what-you-can-do/index.html
Bullying is a serious issue at schools around the world. This list of resources sheds light on topics related to bullying in educational settings.

https://www.time4learning.com/testprep/
This website presents a list of standardized tests used in states across the nation.

http://www.nea.org/tools/special-education-IDEA-resources.html
Here you will find a list of resources for parents of children with special needs and disabilities.

# CHAPTER NOTES

[1] Nelson Mandela, quoted in Valerie Strauss, "Nelson Mandela on the power of education," *Washington Post* (December 5, 2013). https://www.washingtonpost.com/news/answer-sheet/wp/ 2013/12/05/nelson-mandelas-famous-quote-on-education/?utm_term=.0b43b9e3d76c

[2] Malcolm X, speech at the Founding Rally of the Organization of Afro-American Unity," (1964). https://blackpast.org/1964-malcolm-x-s-speech-founding-rally-organization-afro-american-unity

[3] Elaine Hom, "What is STEM Education?," *Live Science* (February 2014). https://www.live-science.com/43296-what-is-stem-education.html

[4] Ken Robinson, "How Schools Kill Creativity," TED (February 2006). https://www.ted.com/ talks/ken_robinson_says_schools_kill_creativity?language=en

[5] Donalyn Miller, *The Book Whisperer: Awakening the Inner Reader in Every Child* (San Francisco: Jossey-Bass, 2009), p.166.

[6] Susanna Loeb, "Teacher quality: Improving teacher quality and distribution," National Academy of Education Policy White Paper Series (2008). https://cepa.stanford.edu/content/teacher-quality-improving-teacher-quality-and-distribution

[7] Anne Podolsky, Tara Kini, Joseph Bishop, and Linda Darling-Hammond, "Solving the Teacher Shortage: How to Attract and Retain Excellent Educators," Learning Policy Institute (September 2016). https://learningpolicyinstitute.org/product/solving-teacher-shortage-brief

[8] Marta W. Aldrich, "How do you improve schools? Start by coaching principals, says new study," *Chalkbeat* (August 2018). https://chalkbeat.org/posts/tn/2018/08/10/how-do-you-improve-schools-start-by-coaching-principals-says-new-study/

[9] Alexis Cox, "More than half of US public schools need repairs, survey finds," PBS (March 2014). https://www.pbs.org/newshour/education/half-u-s-public-schools-need-repairs-modernization-survey-finds

[10] OJJDP Statistical Briefing Book, "Juvenile violent crime time of day," (accessed October 16, 2018). https://www.ojjdp.gov/ojstatbb/offenders/qa03301.asp

[11] Andrew J. Rotherham, "The 3 Main Obstacles in the Way of Education Reform," *The Atlantic* (April 2012). https://www.theatlantic.com/national/archive/2012/04/the-3-main-obstacles-in-the-way-of-education-reform/256144/

[12] Debbie Alexander, Laurie Lewis, and John Ralph, "Condition of America's Public School Facilities, 2012–13," National Center for Education Statistics, US Department of Education (March 2014), p 3. https://nces.ed.gov/pubs2014/2014022.pdf

[13] Cindy Long, "How Do We Increase Teacher Quality in Low-Income Schools?,"

*NEA Today* (May 2011). http://neatoday.org/2011/05/24/how-do-we-increase-teacher-quality-at-low-income-schools/

14 Bill Gates, "Bill Gates: Commend Common Core," *USA Today* (February 2014). https:// www.usatoday.com/story/opinion/2014/02/11/bill-melinda-gates-common-core-education-column/5404469/

15 Jeb Bush, quoted in Kathleen Hennessey, "Jeb Bush's embrace of Common Core is a campaign lightning rod," *LA Times* (August 2015). http://www.latimes.com/nation/politics/la-na-bush-common-core-20150820-story.html

16 Cindy Long, "Six Ways the Common Core is Good For Students," *NEA Today* (May 2013). http://neatoday.org/2013/05/10/six-ways-the-common-core-is-good-for-students-2/

17 Douglas Holtz-Eakin, "A Hidden Benefit to Common Core," *US News* (April 2016). https:// www.usnews.com/news/articles/2016-04-27/common-core-standards-benefit-the-economy

18 David Greene, "The Long Death of Creative Teaching," *US News* (March 2014). https:// www.usnews.com/opinion/articles/2014/03/17/how-common-core-standards-kill-creative-teaching

19 Bureau of Labor Statistics, "69.7 percent of 2016 high school graduates enrolled in college in October 2016" (accessed October 16, 2018). https://www.bls.gov/opub/ted/2017/69-point-7-per-cent-of-2016-high-school-graduates-enrolled-in-college-in-october-2016.htm

20 Joy Pullman, "Estimate: Common Core to Cost California Nearly $10 Billion, Nation $80 Billion," *The Federalist* (January 27, 2016). http://thefederalist.com/2016/01/27/estimate-common-core-to-cost-california-nearly-10-billion-nation-80-billion/

21 Katharine Beals, "The Common Core Is Tough on Kids With Special Needs," *The Atlantic* (February 2014). https://www.theatlantic.com/education/archive/2014/02/the-common-core-is-tough-on-kids-with-special-needs/283973/

22 Maggie Gallagher, "Is a good teacher certifiable?," *Town Hall* (July 2003). https:// townhall.com/columnists/maggiegallagher/2003/07/22/is-a-good-teacher-certifiable-n959484

23 Andrew Cuomo, "State of the State Speech," *New York Times* (January 2016). https://www.nytimes.com/2016/01/14/nyregion/transcript-of-cuomos-2016-state-of-the-state-address.html

24 Karl Zinsmeister, "From Promising to Proven," *Philanthropy* (2014). https://www.philanthropyroundtable.org/philanthropy-magazine/article/spring-2014-from-promising-to-proven

25 Sean Coughlan, "Online schools 'worse than traditional teachers'," BBC (November 2015). https://www.bbc.com/news/business-34671952

# CHAPTER NOTES

26 California Charter Schools Association, "African American Student Performance in Charters" (accessed October 15, 2018). http://www.ccsa.org/understanding/research/africanamericanreport/

27 National Charter School Resource Center, "Fundraising Plays an Important Role at Charter Schools" (accessed October 14, 2018). https://charterschoolcenter.ed.gov/newsletter/ september-2010-fundraising-plays-important-role-charter-schools

28 Education Commission of the States. "Charter Schools: Do teachers in a charter school have to be certified?" (accessed October 14, 2018). http://ecs.force.com/mbdata/mbquestNB2C? rep=CS1720

29 Georgia State University, "Teachers Are Leaving Privately Managed Charter Schools at Alarming Rates" (accessed October 15, 2018). https://news.gsu.edu/2018/08/28/teachers-are-leaving-privately-managed-charter-schools-at-alarming-rates-study-finds/

30 Dave Burgess, *Teach Like a Pirate: Increase Student Engagement, Boost Your Creativity, and Transform Your Life as an Educator* (San Diego: Dave Burgess Consulting, Inc., 2012), p. 141.

31 Barack Obama, "An Open Letter to America's Parents and Teachers: Let's Make Our Testing Smarter," Obama White House (October 2015). https://obamawhitehouse.archives.gov/blog/ 2015/10/26/open-letter-americas-parents-and-teachers-lets-make-our-testing-smarter

32 Ronnie Reese, "Minority Testing Bias Persists," *Huff Post* (December 2017). https:// www.huffingtonpost.com/ronnie-reese/test-bias-minorities_b_2734149.html

33 FairTest, "Standardized Testing and Students with Disabilities" (accessed October 15, 2018). https://www.fairtest.org/standardized-testing-and-students-disabilities

34 Lynn Olson, "Study Questions Reliability of Single-Year-Test-Score Gains," *Education Week* (May 2001). https://www.edweek.org/ew/articles/2001/05/23/37brookings.h20.html

35 Erik Robelen, "How Much Testing Is Too Much?," *The Atlantic* (June 2016). https://www.theatlantic.com/education/archive/2016/06/how-much-testing-is-too-much/485633/

36 Greg Toppo, "Survey: Nearly half of teachers would quit now for higher-paying job," *USA Today* (May 2016). https://www.usatoday.com/story/news/2016/05/05/nearly-half-teachers-would-quit-now-higher-paying-job/83975714/

37 Knight Foundation, "Survey Finds Teaching to the Test has Negative Impact On Use of News in Classrooms: Carnegie-Knight Task Force Urges More Emphasis on Civics Education," (accessed October 15, 2018). https://knightfoundation.

org/press/releases/survey-finds-teaching-to-the-test-has-negative

[38] Gregory J. Cizek, "Unintended Consequences of High Stakes Testing—P-12," *Educational Measurement: Issues and Practice* (September 2001). http://physicsed.buffalostate.edu/pubs/ STANYS/Nov03/Assessment/Resources%20 NYSED)/cizekreport.htm

[39] Valerie Straus, "How and why convicted Atlanta teachers cheated on standardized tests," *Washington Post* (April 2015). https://www.washingtonpost.com/news/answer-sheet/wp/ 2015/04/01/how-and-why-convicted-atlanta-teachers-cheated-on-standardized-tests/?utm_term=. 073a65a436a9

[40] Andrew Ujifusa, "Standardized Testing Costs States $1.7 Billion a Year, Study Says," *Education Week* (November 2012). https://www.edweek.org/ew/articles/2012/11/29/13testcosts.h32.html

[41] Dennis Owens, "Do standardized tests work and are they worth the cost?," ABC (April 2017). https://www.abc27.com/news/do-standardized-tests-work-and-are-they-worth-the-cost/ 1036999755

[42] Sam Dillon, "Top Test Scores from Shanghai Stun Educators," *New York Times* (December 2010). https://www.nytimes.com/2010/12/07/education/07education.html

[43] Philip Elliott and Jennifer Agiesta, "AP-NORC Poll: Parents back high-stakes testing ," AP-NORC (August 2013). http://www.apnorc.org/news-media/Pages/News+Media/ap-norc-poll-parents-back-high-stakes-testing.aspx

[44] Brian Scios, "Where's the Backlash? Students Say They Don't Fret Standardized Tests," Public Agenda (March 2002). https://www.publicagenda.org/press-releases/wheres-backlash-students-say-they-dont-fret-standardized-tests

[45] Louis V. Gerstner Jr., "The Tests We Know We Need," *The New York Times* (March 2002). https://www.nytimes.com/2002/03/14/opinion/the-tests-we-know-we-need.html

[46] Brian Scios, "Where's the Backlash? Students Say They Don't Fret Standardized Tests," Public Agenda (March 2002). https://www.publicagenda.org/press-releases/wheres-backlash-students-say-they-dont-fret-standardized-tests

# ORGANIZATIONS TO CONTACT

American Federation of Teachers
555 New Jersey Avenue, NW
Washington, DC 20001
Phone: (202) 879-4400
Website: https://www.aft.org

National Art Education Association
901 Prince Street
Alexandria, VA 22314
Phone: 1-800-299-8321
Fax: 1-703-860-2960
Website: https://www.arteducators.org/
Email: info@arteducators.org

National Association for the Education of
Young Children
1313 L Street, NW, Suite 500
Washington, DC 20005-4104
Phone: 202-232-8777
Website: https://www.naeyc.org/

National Council for the Social Studies
8555 Sixteenth Street, Suite 500
Silver Spring, MD 20910
Phone: (301) 588-1800
Website: https://www.socialstudies.org/

National Education Association
1201 16th Street, NW
Washington, DC 20036-3290
Phone: (202) 833-4000
Fax: (202) 822-7974
Website: https://www.nea.org

National Parent-Teacher Association
1250 North Pitt Street
Alexandria, VA 22314
Phone: (703) 518-1200
Fax: (703) 836-0942
Website: https://www.pta.org
Email: info@pta.org

Partner Alliance for Safer Schools
Website: https://passk12.org/

United States Distance Learning
Association
840 First Street, NE, 3rd Floor
Washington, DC 20002
Phone: (202) 248-5023
Website: https://www.usdla.org

# INDEX

accountability
  of charter schools, 68, 71, 75
  of education system, 21–22, 29, 99
  Jeb Bush on, 60
  standardized tests and, 99
  of teachers, 31
accreditation, 9
achievement gap, 37–38, 54
Adams, Lewis, 16
Adequate Yearly Progress (AYP), 83
Alaska, 51
art and music programs, 61

Baltimore County public school system, 25
Bentley, Robert, 50
black students, 16–17, 20, 74
Boston Latin school, 12
*Brown v. Board of Education of Topeka, Kansas* (1954), 18–20
Bureau of Labor Statistics, 61
Burgess, Dave, 85
Bush, George W., 21
Bush, Jeb, 60

California, 62–63
character education programs, 23
charter schools
  accountability of, 68, 71, 75
  admission requirements, 68, 73–74, 76–77, 80
  benefits of, 71–74
  definition of, 67–68
  features of, 68–69, 79
  funding of, 68, 70, 74, 75, 77–78
  Milburn schools, 77
  numbers of, 69, 70
  online education in, 72, 73
  opposition to, 75–80
  parents and, 67, 69, 72, 74, 76
  special needs students and, 76
  standardized testing and, 75–76
  teachers in, 71, 79–80
cheating
  by school administrators, 40, 41
  on standardized tests, 93, 99
China, 94
College Entrance Examination Board, 91
colleges
  entrance exams, 90, 91

student readiness for, 55, 57, 61, 98
Common Core curriculum
  benefits of, 54–58
  components of, 49–52, 54
  costs of implementation, 62–63
  definition of, 10, 49
  impact on learning, 52
  mathematics, 52
  opposition to, 51, 52–53, 59–64
  special needs students and, 63–64
  standardized testing and, 53, 64
  standards for, 49, 53, 54, 56
  states implementation of, 50, 51
  teachers and, 54–56, 57–58, 59, 61–62
  writing, 49–51
costs
  of Common Core curriculum implementation, 62–63
  of education system reform, 45–46
  of school building repairs, 45
  of standardized tests, 93
  of teacher compensation, 31–34, 41–43, 45–46
critical thinking skills, 52, 57–58, 61
Cruz, Nikolas, 25
cultural bias and standardized tests, 64, 85–86, 97
Cuomo, Andrew, 78
cursive writing, 51

Delaware, 51

Education for all Handicapped Children Act of 1975, 18, 21
education system
  accountability of, 21–22, 29, 99
  goals of education, 10, 11, 17
  number of schools, 7–8
  number of students, 7
  parental involvement, 45, 58
  *See also* Common Core curriculum; public education; standardized tests and testing; teachers
education system reform
  barriers to, 40–46
  Bill Gates on, 33
  bureaucratic stagnation, 40–41
  class size, 10, 36, 37
  costs of, 45–46

# INDEX

effectiveness of, 30
learning techniques, 37
methods of, 29, 31–39
political impact on, 43, 45
research on, 29–30, 34, 39
school buildings and, 38–39, 45
*See also* Common Core curriculum; public education; standardized tests and testing; teachers
Elementary and Secondary Education Act of 1965, 20–21
Eliot, Charles William, 91
Every Student Succeeds Act of 2015, 22–23, 83–84

female students, 12, 15
funding
of charter schools, 68, 70, 74, 75, 77–78
for school building repairs, 38, 39
for special education, 19
for STEM, 23

Gallagher, Maggie, 69
Gates, Bill, 33, 55, 77–78
Gates, Melinda, 77–78
Global Education Index, 8
Gray, Adam, 43

Harvard University, 12, 91
Higher Education Act of 1955, 21
homeschooling, 9, 12–13

individualized education plan (IEP), 19
Individuals with Disabilities Education Act of 1990, 18, 76

Johnson administration, 20–21

laws
Education for all Handicapped Children Act of 1975, 18, 21
Elementary and Secondary Education Act of 1965, 20–21
Every Student Succeeds Act of 2015, 22–23, 83–84
Higher Education Act of 1955, 21
Individuals with Disabilities Education Act of 1990, 18, 76

No Child Left Behind Act of 2002, 21–22, 83

Malcolm X, 17
Mandela, Nelson, 11
Mann, Horace, 14, 15–16
March for Our Lives, 24
Marjory Stoneman Douglas High School (Parkland, FL) shooting, 24, 25
Massachusetts Bay colony, 12
mathematics in Common Core, 52
*See also* STEM
Milburn charter schools, 77
Miller, Donalyn, 32
Minnesota, 51
Mount Holyoke College, 15
music and art programs, 61

National Assessment of Educational Progress, 56
National Center for Education Statistics, 19, 45
National Center for Fair and Open Testing, 87
New Jersey, 26
No Child Left Behind Act of 2002, 21–22, 83

Oakland (CA), 46
Obama, Barack, 88
Obama administration, 23

Pagourtzis, Dimitrios, 25
parents
character education programs and, 23
charter schools and, 67, 69, 72, 74, 76
homeschooling and, 9, 12, 13
involvement in education system, 45, 58
school choice and, 64, 67, 94
support for standardized testing, 94–96
Pell Grants, 21
Pennsylvania, 93
primary schools, 10
principals, 35, 36
private schools vs. public schools, 8–9
public education
history of, 12–22
primary schools, 10
public schools vs. private, 8–9
secondary schools, 11

# INDEX

*See also* Common Core curriculum; education system; education system reform; standardized tests and testing

resource officers, 25, 26
Robinson, Ken, 42

Santa Fe High School (Santa Fe, TX) shooting, 24, 25
SBAC, 87
school buildings
 numbers of, 7–8
 repairs of, 38, 39, 45
 safety and, 25–26, 39
"school choice," 64, 67, 94
school shootings, 24, 25–26
Science, Technology, Engineeing, and Math curriculum. *See* STEM curriculum
secondary schools, 11
security measures in schools, 25–26
segregation, 16–20
Shanghai, 94
Smarter Balanced Assessment Consortium (SBAC), 87
special education
 funding for, 19
 laws requiring, 18, 21
 numbers of students, 19
special needs students
 charter schools and, 76
 Common Core curriculum and, 63–64
 individualized education plan, 19
 standardized tests and, 86, 87, 98–99
standardized tests and testing
 accountability of, 99
 charter schools and, 75–76
 cheating on, 93, 99
 Common Core curriculum and, 53, 64
 confidentiality of, 96–97
 costs of, 93
 cultural bias and, 64, 85–86, 97
 effectiveness of, 92, 93, 96
 history of, 90, 91
 international use of, 94
 parental support of, 94–96
 problems with, 84–93
 purpose of, 83
 research on, 88, 89–90, 91, 93, 95, 97, 98
 skills assessed, 84, 87–88, 91, 97–98

special needs students and, 86, 87, 98–99
 support for, 84, 94–99
 teachers and, 89–90, 91, 93, 95–96, 97
 test anxiety, 89, 92–93, 96–97, 98
 use in professional licensing, 98
STEM curriculum, 22, 23, 52
student to teacher ratio, 36, 37

Teacher of the Year award, 43
teachers
 accountability of, 31
 African-American, 16
 in charter schools, 71, 79–80
 Common Core curriculum and, 54–56, 57–58, 59, 61–62
 compensation for, 31–34, 41–43, 45–46
 morale of, 90
 non-financial support for, 34, 36
 ratio to students, 36, 37
 standardized testing and, 89–90, 91, 93, 95–96, 97
 teachers unions and, 41–44
 training for, 31
 turnover rate of, 30
 working conditions of, 34, 35, 43
 *See also* education system; education system reform
"teaching to the test," 59–60, 89, 91, 97
test anxiety, 89, 92–93, 96–97, 98
Trends in International Mathematics and Science Study, 56
Tuskegee Institute, 16

universities. *See* colleges
US Department of Education, 23
US Supreme Court decisions, 18–20

virtual charter schools, 72, 73
 *See also* charter schools

Washington, Booker T., 16
Washington, D.C., 39, 40, 41
Webster, Noah, 13
writing in Common Core curriculum, 49–51

# AUTHOR'S BIOGRAPHY AND CREDITS

## ABOUT THE AUTHOR

Ashley Nicole is an author and true crime writer with a background in psychology and sociology. Though a California native, she currently lives in Arizona, where she enjoys hiding from the sun and writing novels.

## PICTURE CREDITS

Bureau of Alcohol, Tobacco, Firearms, and Explosives: 42; Everett Historical: 18; Federal Bureau of Investigation: 32, 66; Jefferson County Sheriff's Office: 64; Library of Congress: 20; Ronald Reagan Presidential Library: 24; used under license from Shutterstock, Inc.: 10, 11, 12, 28, 40, 60, 71, 76, 82; 3000 ad / Shutterstock.com: 50; Yasemin Yurtman Candemir: 30; Evenfh / Shutterstock.com: 8; Sheila Fitzgerald / Shutterstock.com: 88; James Gabbert / Shutterstock.com: 84; Juli Hansen / Shutterstock.com: 94; Keith Homan / Shutterstock.com: 37; A. Katz / Shutterstock.com: 68, 81; Melissamn / Shutterstock.com: 6; Lev Radin / Shutterstock.com: 98; Janos Rautonen / Shutterstock.com: 53; Mark Reinstein / Shutterstock.com: 96; Crush Rush / Shutterstock.com: 97; Rena Schild / Shutterstock.com: 75, 91; Albert H. Teich / Shutterstock.com: 46; Perris Tumbao / Shutterstock.com: 54; Leonard Zhukovsky / Shutterstock.com: 62; US House of Representatives: 27.